A Clearer Path to Divorce

How she prepared for divorce with financial, professional, and emotional support

Nanette Murphy

Live Life Now LLC

Dedicated to…

All the women who have supported, guided, and encouraged me on this journey.

And to the woman reading this guide today who needs the guidance and support inside this book. You are strong enough to reach out for help.

YOU'VE GOT THIS.

"Strength is what we gain from the
madness we survive."

– HNasty

Contents

A Letter to the Reader

To the woman preparing for her next chapter, you get to write this one.

I am sorry that you need the information contained in these pages, but I am thrilled you are reading this book. You have taken that first step to ensure you are informed and prepared for the process ahead of you.

I wrote this book intending to help you because I would have significantly benefited from a book like this—one that would have guided me and given me hope, inspiration, and insight into what lies ahead through the divorce process.

The journey you are about to go on can make you feel alone, isolated, and fearful of the future. I am here to tell you that you will be okay.

I am here to walk beside you on this journey, one step at a time.

Wishing you peace, happiness, and love,

Nanette Murphy

Introduction

We all recall 2020, whether we were stuck on the sofa, binging Netflix and cookies or panicking about safety and an uncertain future.

After about a week of quarantine, I decided I needed to be productive. Taking control and learning something new would help me deal with all the uncertainty I couldn't control. Granted, most of the world felt the same way, hence the great bread making trend of 2020.

Yale University was offering some free online courses, so I began looking into what they had to offer, and The Science of Well-Being sounded intriguing. The world had changed our daily routines, and that upheaval threatened everyone's well-being.

Just one free Yale University class helped me get to where I am today, as a published author, speaker, divorce & health coach for women.

During that class, the professor referred to Dr. Michael Beckwith. His name rang a bell, so I turned to Google and researched him during my abundance of spare time. His dreadlocks were gone; in fact, he was now bald and a little older, but I remembered Oprah interviewing Dr. Beckwith, who is a spiritual leader and teacher, author, guide for meditation, and more. Through my research of Dr. Beckwith, I discovered his Mindvalley program. This discovery was life changing. I immediately signed up for Dr. Beckwith's program, which offers courses on meditation; self-care; hypnotherapy; life coaching; and the mind, body, and soul. The list is endless. I learned so much from him and others within the community who gave me insight and direction. I couldn't get enough of all this program offered.

One practice I began was meditation, which I had struggled with before, primarily because I had never given it the time needed. But with Mindvalley's methods and instruction, I learned how to relax, concentrate on my breathing and learned different methods of meditation. I think I was able to focus and learn because life slowed down. And through meditation and reflection, I discovered I wanted to become a life coach.

I prayed and reflected and knew I needed to do this.

Once again, my old friend Google led me to the John Maxwell Team, a coaching certification program. I spoke with an advisor and liked the program, so once again I dove in.

My mornings were filled with exercise, meditation, and a class—but in whatever order the spirit moved me that day. I even went so far as printing business cards before I was certified. This was my way of manifesting what I wanted.

Sadly, because of COVID (there I said it), I had to earn my certification via a virtual event in March 2021. In the meantime, my course instructor encouraged us all to start coaching and to get a life coach for ourselves. This was intended for us to learn from them. Many coaches have coaches of their own. We all need support and guidance.

What would our lives be without Google? My internet research yielded a couple of ladies whom I interviewed, and I made a great connection with one in particular. I signed up with her for six coaching sessions. I wasn't sure what to expect as I assumed I knew I was on the right path.

I never expected what would happen next. In our first session, our conversation unfolded, and she discovered that one of my goals was to write a memoir. Suddenly, she was quizzing me.

"Do you know how long it takes to write a book?" she asked.

"No," I said.

"Do you know how long the average book is?"

"No."

"Have you started writing your book?"

"I have a few words down," I said.

She continued, "When do you plan on writing this book?"

"I think when my coaching business is up and running?"

"Why are you waiting?"

I had no good answer. But what she said next flipped a switch.

"You know your story could be the cornerstone of your life coaching business?"

I knew I couldn't wait anymore. It was time to start writing and why not. What else did I have to do?
Even though the world had shut down, I had a desk, a laptop, and a chair. Away I went. My fingers flew across the keyboard. Each time she and I met, I shared my accompaniments from the previous two weeks and had

another timeline for the number of words I had to pour out onto the screen.

Sometimes I felt stuck. I didn't know what pieces to share about my story of heartbreak, healing, and growth. Sometimes memories surfaced that I hadn't thought of in years. But my coach helped me to stay focused and complete my writing. The goal of my memoir was not to hurt anyone, including myself. I was not writing my story to dwell in the past. I wanted my story to inspire, encourage, and help the reader through their dark times. I knew I had knowledge and experience to offer and share and I wanted to do something bigger than I had ever dreamed.

As I wrote, a sense of accomplishment filled me—not only because I was on a journey to becoming a published author but also because I could see more clearly how far I had come from the darkest days of my life, through my healing, and ultimately my growth into a stronger, happier version of myself. And my growth continues.

I completed my memoir in about six months. I worked with an editor and eventually a publishing company.

In August 2021, I finally published *Shattered Dreams & New Beginnings: A journey of heartbreak, growth, and new beginnings.*

While publishing my book marked a new milestone for me, I had celebrated another breakthrough moment just a few months prior. In early 2021, I was approached to be a part of a team of coaches: divorce coaches. As I shared in my memoir, I had been divorced since 2015, after more than 20 years of marriage. That divorce plummeted me into a sad, dark, and depressing time in my life. A dark time that lasted two years. I only wish I had known there was such a thing as a divorce coach.

But back then, I couldn't fathom how my life would change, how I'd find my purpose when I emerged from that darkness, how I'd find myself and happiness again. I couldn't picture such a future because all I saw were my previous plans, the ones I thought guaranteed, crumbling around me.

We began our lives together in our mid-twenties. It was the 80's: I had big hair, and he had big dreams. Being a mother was what I wanted most. He was driven, intelligent, and determined to be successful. We both came from humble beginnings. My husband and I remained close to our extended families, both of whom also enjoyed being together, so we often celebrated special occasions as one huge family. It was ideal. Money was tight, but we never fought about that.

Young and in love, we married after dating for five years. We bought a little white house with a flat roof and a big backyard in a city near where I grew up. The neighborhood and house were perfect for a young couple beginning their life together. A couple of years later, we had our first daughter, and I experienced a new kind of unconditional love in this beautiful baby girl.

A year and a half later, our lives began to shift. His job took us to another country, from Canada to the United States. I was reluctant, nervous, and scared. But I knew he wanted this, and I had to go. He was the only one earning an income, and his new job would help our family out financially.

We lived about an hour from each of our families, which left me feeling isolated and lonely. Our new home was in Michigan. I was a nice, and we had lovely neighbors, but I didn't have much in common with them. And everyone had so much acreage and trees that we couldn't see other houses. As a young mother in a new area, a new country in fact, I couldn't seem to adjust.

I do not know how I got through this complete shift in my life and the loss of having our extended family nearby. But I had strength that I was not even aware of, and I had a little girl to raise. Then our family grew again. Our son was a joy, a little man with spunk and smiles.

It was an adjustment as my husband worked hard but was not content. I wanted to raise our family and grow as a family together. He wanted a better job with a more important position.

In short, my husband and I struggled to make do with our situation. Then one crisp fall day in 1995, about a year after our son was born, my husband and I were in the yard with the kids. Our daughter was playing, and my son was in his stroller. We were doing yard work when my husband then turned to me and announced that he wanted to move to another state.

Without hesitation, I said, "Where, where, where?" That's how much I disliked our current location.

He had already researched our options and listed two possible states, but he let me make the final choice: California! He had found jobs in each state. I don't recall what the other state was.

This new adventure began a life I never expected. It didn't happen overnight, but success was building for our whole family, both financially and internally. Not only did I begin to flourish again, but my husband and I also grew as a couple as we had new friends, new places to explore, and new restaurants to try.

Two years later, my husband was building a successful new company, and California almost felt like home. Despite all the fun we had exploring the area, we knew that California living was not for us. It had always been a temporary stay. He loved hunting, fishing and golf and that was not the place to do all of that. I missed living in a house with a yard for the kids to play in and being close to family.

We also anticipated having another child, and I wanted to be closer to our families before that happened, so I had a new outlook when we decided to return to Michigan.

We moved back to Michigan and soon after we had a new baby on the way but also had registered our oldest daughter for school. Life continued to bring about changes as my husband's business grew. In fact, his success snowballed, which excited us all.

Soon, we didn't have to worry about money, which brought on a feeling of comfort but also a fast-paced life. We joined a golf and country club that I had no desire to visit—in addition to making new "friends" and building a new home that took up too much of our time—all while trying to maintain a normal life for our children. It did make my head spin at times.

Keeping up with my husband was always challenging. He would get an idea, ponder it, weigh the pros and cons, and then inform me what he wanted to do once he decided to act on it. His ideas weren't a joint decision; I just had to be on board. I always caught up, but I never knew what was next, which made raising a family challenging.

We had a great life, not without challenges, but no one's life is without complications and troubles.

My husband's successful business eventually allowed him to retire early. We lived in a magnificent home, traveled, and often entertained while life unfolded. Our kids were teenagers and young adults. While navigating a new status in life, I always managed to stay grounded. I say this confidently as my closest friends always confirm that with me.

My husband, not so much. He was generous, always had a new plan or idea, and didn't leave much room for family time. I eventually learned that was the least of our problems.

All his money and free time left me feeling alone, neglected, and eventually frustrated.

One day, we were out to lunch at our favorite local sushi bar. We had finished eating, and I was enjoying our time together. But then his phone rang, and before we had paid the bill, he had made plans to golf and was off to join his friends for a spur of the moment golf game. He left me sitting at the table, waiting for the check. I guess I drove myself home, I don't recall. I do know this is a pivotal point for me. I was not important to him.

I felt myself growing away from him. I was tired of being second to everything. We had a few months of real struggles. Mainly because I was not giving in to him. You know when you and your spouse argue and then there may be a few hours of the "silent treatment" Well we went through a long patch of those moments. Why? Because I was always the one breaking the silence. I was always the one saying "sorry" and I had run out of *sorries*. During this time, he began to realize that he may actually have to put effort into our marriage, and he did.

For our twentieth anniversary, he planned a surprise trip for us to celebrate in Paris. We had never celebrated like this before, and I was on a high from that trip for weeks afterward. We had gotten through our troubling times from earlier that year. At least, that is how it seemed.

However, hindsight is real; I didn't see then that he had squeezed our Paris trip in between his guy trips. By our twenty-first anniversary, we had hit rock bottom.

My intuition told me something was wrong. He was more distant than ever. I felt I knew what the problem was and even though I was not ready to face the truth, I pursued the information I needed. It was just after our Twenty-first wedding anniversary. No words can describe that moment. Infidelity: the word that broke my world and shook me to the core.

I wanted to unhear what I had heard from a reliable source, and that was impossible.

Have you ever broken anything? Of course, you have. A dish? It crashes to the floor, and the shards of glass scatter everywhere. Maybe a bone? You feel the pain throughout your entire body, and it takes your breath away. You can throw out broken items or replace them. A broken bone requires a cast and about six to eight weeks of healing. You may move awkwardly for a few weeks, but you recover.

What about a broken heart?

First, you feel numb, like your heart has stopped; you aren't sure it's still pumping. Then, it slowly feels empty but also heavy. This weight inside you causes indescribable pain.

Living in denial is not easy, because deep down I knew I couldn't live with this information.

I tried to live and act as I did before this devasting news slammed into my ears and circled my brain. I did try. But I fooled no one—not my friends; not my family; and worse of all, not my children. Just myself.

There is no band aid. There is not enough sunshine, laughter, or friends and family to heal you. You prefer to be alone. Retreating inward is just a natural action; there is nothing anyone can do for you. No words can heal your broken heart, and the pain runs deep. You move through the days automatically.

I was a mother and had a household to run; I also kept a secret. I never realized that keeping a secret this big and this disturbing could eat away at the soul. I was not fond of nighttime, so I ensured I kept liquid courage in the house to numb my pain and help me sleep. For a brief moment in the morning—you know, those few seconds between deep sleep and waking up—those few fleeting moments each morning were all the peace I had in my heart. Then, in an instant, reality woke up too. I was living in the ugly truth again. I felt trapped in my sadness and paralyzed, unable to completely accept where my marriage had ended.

Two years was how long I lived in denial. First, my husband's infidelity crippled me. But it was a double-edged sword; the mistress was my friend.

I had always said I would tolerate anything but infidelity in my marriage; I had said that easily, confidently, because I *never* thought it would happen. But that impossibility had become real. And now I had to follow through, stand my ground, and take action.

But how could I? It takes a while to let it all sink in. Enough time passes, and you begin to understand that things aren't going to improve. Lies continued, and I eventually uncovered more of the truth. It took months to admit that three people in a marriage doesn't work. Living under these circumstances was demeaning, disrespectful, and cruel.

After I accepted that he was no longer the man I had married and I had reached the end of my rope, I started gaining my self-respect back. Thankfully I eventually admitted that I had to move forward with my life.

As much as I struggled to reach this point, I realized my heart had not been completely torn to pieces in that tornado of sadness and disappointment. There was a small piece left. I realized it was growing again because I had begun to nurture it. I was taking care of myself and focusing on healing. This was ultimately the best decision for the kids as well. They all knew it as well.

Divorce was the only next move.

I began learning that healing is an active process. Healing doesn't magically wrap you up in a soft cloak and transform you. Nope! Healing is not going to happen that way.

You can't give up. You dig deep for strength, which builds your determination. And that determination gets you out of the darkness you live in. Yes, it gets very dark. You can't see reality. But, like anything, you see a dim light when you keep moving forward. That light gets brighter. Then, the sun does shine again. You find the courage to keep building your strength.

Holding onto my determination was challenging as the days, weeks, and years went by, but learning to rely on myself was an essential chapter in my healing and growing process. Choosing to move out of my marital home was my first step. The home we took years to build. The home I looked after. The home I decorated room by room. Each interior detail made our house warm and welcoming even before our belongings added the final touches. But I was ready to let go so I could finally move forward without the past lingering around me.

I found a house that I loved and created a new, warm, and welcoming home. My youngest daughter moved there with me. My son lived between his dad's house and mine, and my oldest had moved away a couple of years prior.

We lived in this home for three years. My children and I filled it with good times like birthday celebrations, girlfriend holiday parties were some of wonderful gatherings. Times I hold precious in my memory. These Beautiful moments were part of my healing. These important moments assisted in building my confidence and strength. Continuing to do the things that were important to me before. I learned to get to know the woman looking back at me in the mirror each morning. She is pretty awesome.

Healing doesn't run into you and knock you down like heartbreak does.

No, healing approaches you gently. If you actively allow it to come. For me, the healing process unfolded by making some new friends and entertaining again, something I loved to do. Self-care became a massive part of my life. Quiet moments in a space I created that was tranquil. Adult coloring helped me sit peacefully and meditation. I traveled with a friend, visited my daughter in another state. I began volunteering at a local shelter for women and children, and that put my life in perspective. It made me more aware of how wonderful my life still was. It was just different. I still had tears at times, but even those dark days began to disappear.

Dating was not my thing, but I did meet a man I fell in love with. Meeting at a mutual friend's retirement party. I wasn't looking for a partner, I never intended to remarry, but never say never.

I was living life and enjoying myself. However, I knew I still had something else to do throughout this journey. I didn't know what that was, but I've learned that life has a way of working out.

You may need help navigating the path, but the further along you get, the why becomes clearer. You just have to take those steps, one at a time—because you never know when you will register for a random, free class (during a pandemic, no less) that will lead you toward your new purpose.

Chapter 1

Hiring Your Team of Professionals

Welcome to your guidelines on divorce recommendations. This chapter covers hiring the professionals you need, including how to find them, what questions to ask, and what to watch out for. I like to peg it as hiring your posse of people.

Most people think they immediately need to hire a divorce attorney, and you eventually do, but that really is not the first person you need to hire. You need to hire a few other professionals first who will complete the puzzle and ensure your success. Qualified professionals who not only specialize in divorce cases but also will assist you emotionally and advise you financially are important to have in your corner while you are preparing for divorce. Together they can give you peace of mind and make the process go as smoothly as possible.

Divorce coaches

The first person you should hire is a divorce coach. They understand the moving pieces of the processes will save you from a giant headache. They will give you insight, knowledge, and guidance through the process. Having somebody you can count on for emotional support and who has answers to questions that you are not sure of is huge. This entire process is going to be stressful, and you might find yourself being less organized than usual. You are going to have a lot of people to hire and a lot of hoops to jump through, so delegating a lot of this to a qualified professional is an essential place to start. To ensure everything goes smoothly, hire somebody who has been through a divorce and who can help you remain focused.

The importance of a divorce coach is one that I recommend based on personal experience. When I went through my divorce, I had a counselor, but I did not have somebody who was well versed in the entire process of divorce. As a result, I stretched myself too thin and had to deal with additional negative impacts on my mental and physical health. Having somebody who could have helped shoulder the burden and direct me toward the right people would have taken so much pressure off me. The great news is that you do not have to make the same mistake, and I have your back. A divorce coach will also be able to help prepare you for issues and challenges you don't even know are coming. For example, most of my clients don't know about Certified Divorce Financial Advisors. I will go into more details about that in the following section. Every woman I talk to who has been divorced says the same thing, "I wish I would have had a Divorce Coach." No kidding, all of them.

Financial advisors

Next, hire a certified divorce financial advisor (CDFA) to oversee your finances. This will essentially be your financial resource throughout the divorce process. Having somebody handle your finances in a time of financial instability will ensure that you are able to sustain your livelihood during this turbulent time. Look for somebody who has experience with divorces and knows the ins and outs of complicated legal matters that can impact finances.

One of the most common misconceptions regarding divorce is that the divorce attorney is the most important person you will hire. However, a CDFA is equally important. They can help you reach a settlement with your attorney, as well as help you with every aspect of the financial settlement that you get from your divorce. A CDFA knows every tax code and short-term and long-term strategies to prevent you from being in a bad financial position post-divorce.

One key feature CDFAs offer is developing a budget for you and stretching your finances as far as possible. This may sound like an easy task for you to manage, but you may be bouncing between jobs or looking for a stable form of employment. No matter what you are facing, you will want to follow the advice of CDFAs, because they will make sure that during this time of instability, you are at the very least financially stable.

I advise that you hire your financial advisor before the divorce process starts, because hiring them early can ensure you spend less time with your attorney. Before the process gets into full swing and attorneys begin volleying financial packages back and forth, CDFAs can lay out your finances and make sure that the split works in your favor.

Divorce attorneys

A divorce attorney is a no-brainer, but hiring the right one can be challenging, as not all divorce attorneys are created equal. Make sure to hire one that has your best interests in mind.

Seek out an attorney who makes themselves accessible to you, as some attorneys are known for not giving you the time of day for a few days at a time. Their apathy will cause you to feel like your case is not important and make you anxious about whether you made the right choice, considering your entire life hinges on the outcome of your attorney's efforts.

The best place to start looking for an attorney is asking friends and family. Reviews online are one thing but having somebody who has used a specific attorney for these types of cases can give you insight into whether that attorney will be a fit for you. Any help you receive from friends and family will better help you to find the right attorney.

If you ask around and cannot find an attorney who is a fit for you, the best place you can go is to reputable review platforms and begin doing research. The internet offers a lot of information that will help you to find an attorney who is well respected by their clients and successful.

When hiring your divorce attorney from a source outside of family and friends, first look at the attorneys' websites and get a feel for what they do differently from each other. Make sure they have adapted to the modern world, because some attorneys haven't furthered their education in order to keep themselves up to speed. For example, if they got their degree in 1990 and have no other certificates, then you should keep searching for another attorney. If their website checks out, that is the first indicator that they are reliable and have been getting a steady stream of clients.

The next thing you are going to want to look at is their experience. You do not want somebody fresh out of law school who will be going up against an attorney with 20 years of divorce cases under their belt. You might end up paying for that mismatch when it comes time to divide the assets. Make sure the attorneys you are reviewing are qualified, have had their fair share of cases, and have gotten their clients what they deserve. This is no time to be the guinea pig, because you are setting up your future.

Each attorney should have a bio that you can read to get a feel for their qualifications. If they say that they specialize in immigration law, they are not likely to be the best choice for a divorce. You want an attorney who specializes in divorce and has a great history of success to propel your case forward and get what you deserve. Be careful of red flags in the bios, and make sure you pay attention to details. The school they went to should not be a degree mill that hands out certificates to anyone who enrolls in their program. Make sure the attorneys have passed the bar for your state and went to a reputable school that will have taught them the intricacies that could be used to your advantage.

Gender bias is also something that you will want to be aware of. If you are a woman and the attorney is a man, the attorney might not connect with you on a philosophical level, which could result in conflicting gender biases. I am not trying to be sexist; however, getting a same-gender attorney will usually alleviate any bias that could be at play. The attorney may not mean to be biased, but bias is not always intentional.

Hire an attorney whom you relate to and have a good working relationship with. They should be someone who understands your goals moving forward with your life and can structure everything to your best advantage. When a divorce attorney does not understand the values of the client they are serving, it can lead to different priorities when negotiating the divorce. Having an attorney who sees eye to eye with you and who identifies with your points of pain will allow them to work as though your divorce was their own. They will usually be able to deliver you a fair split, and both you and the attorney will end up happy.

Hopefully you have enough information to select a few candidates who would be ideal to handle your case. Try and choose three potential candidates, and make sure you conduct interviews. The interview process will allow you to further screen these candidates and to get a feel for exactly which one is right for you.

You are going to want to ask each candidate a few questions. The first is how payment is expected. Ideally, you will want to pay them at the end, considering you want to keep as many liquid assets as possible in your account prior to the process being completed. Liquid assets are assets that can easily be exchanged for cash. Make sure to find out about this, so no surprises come up.

Next, find out if the attorneys expect a bonus at the end of the case. Some attorneys expect to be paid extra if they win the case and get you a great deal. Find out the details, as a bonus could either work in your favor or against you, depending on what they define as a bonus. Agreeing prior to the start of the case on a suitable bonus can help to eliminate surprises. The incentive at the end can also encourage them to maximize their attention on the case.

Last, find out if the consultation is free or if there is a fee. This will give you a better understanding of how the attorney operates and if they will charge you for each interaction. Still, you should ask if the attorney charges for every phone call and email. Find an attorney who doesn't bill for petty things.

Hiring the right attorney is a delicate process that you need to take seriously so that you get the most out of your divorce.

Specialized Realtors

The next part of the team you will want is a realtor. This is not going to be a run of the mill realtor, because the circumstances are much different. You are going to want to hire one who has dealt with selling houses while a divorce is taking place. The realtor needs this special ability because selling and buy homes during a divorce is a highly emotional situation where two parties have a lot at stake. You and your ex will probably argue, so a realtor who can roll through the punches and do what is best for both parties is essential.

Another reason you need a specific realtor on your team is because during the divorce process, unique situations can take place where the realtor will have to know exactly what to do. They need to know how to sell quickly and for the best price possible in order to not stall out the divorce process. This requires an exceptional understanding of market conditions to get the perfect balance of selling on your timeline without sacrificing the income from the sale.

The realtor will also need to be able to act as an intermediary between you and your spouse. Divorces tend to come with high emotions, so the realtor will need to be able to deal with that. The less emotionally they can involve themselves, the better.

Realtors who specialize in helping to sell property during the divorce process are often able to help the individuals involved find a compromise that allows them to move the process forward. This specific type of realtor has the skills needed to meet the demands of both parties at hand and find a resolution. This compromise could be anything from the final sale price to what is included in the sale of the home. Thus, you need to trust that this person will get you the best possible price and can balance the emotional turmoil between you and your spouse.

Forensic Accountant

I highly recommend hiring an accountant to oversee the divorce process. Specifically, hiring a forensic accountant can help track what your spouse is doing with their investments. Being this thorough will ensure your spouse doesn't bury funds into accounts that cannot be traced, which could end up hanging you out to dry. These accountants know how to dig through the finances of your spouse and can track where and when they decide to move money. I have heard countless stories of hundreds of thousands in assets moved into new accounts with no proof, and the other party ended up getting virtually nothing.

A good forensic accountant will not let this happen to you. They will be in your corner and allow you to get exactly what you deserve, while keeping a close eye on your spouse's investments and spending. They are especially important to have onboard for cases that have lot of assets at stake and can often find hidden money. Given that most relationships have one partner who focused more on the finances than the other, having a forensic accountant can be a huge benefit as they ensure all financial assets are accounted for and divided appropriately.

Where to Start

A divorce includes a lot of moving pieces, so you will want a team that makes sure your divorce goes smoothly. When combined, these professionals create a unit working toward getting the best result for you and making sure you are set once the divorce is complete.

Hiring and managing these individuals can be stressful and keep you up at night. You may wonder if you have made the right selections and gave yourself the best path forward. Take it one step at a time and hire one person at a time.

More importantly, hiring this team doesn't have to be another hurdle you have to fight to overcome. Instead, you can make the entire process a positive step forward, and it all starts with your first hire: a divorce coach.

A good divorce coach will support you as you hire the rest of the team. Because they will have gone through the process many times, they can supply you with the appropriate questions to ask, set your expectations for each team member, and provide invaluable insight into how you can help your team all work together to get you the best outcome. A divorce coach will save you a lot of time and money and help you create a trustworthy team that is able to get what you deserve.

I know all too well the uncertainty that accompanies divorce. But remembering that turbulent period of my life inspired me to learn every detail about the divorce process so that I can help others to overcome the pain, confusion, and overwhelm that I faced by myself. If you are feeling alone and confused and about to undergo this difficult journey, you can rely on coaches like me who are ready to help you through the entire process.

Chapter 2

Budgets, Expenses, and Income

The absolute goal is to be able to keep your lifestyle intact throughout and after divorce. Thus, you need to know your finances like your future depends on it, because it absolutely does.

In this chapter, I will cover budgeting, expenses, and your income. This chapter is extremely important for you as a woman. Did you know statistics show that women who have a huge lump sum of money at the end of their divorce are broke within five years because they do not manage their money properly? I do not want that to happen to you.

Know and budget your expenses

You will **not** go broke if you educate yourself. Ask your financial advisor questions and for advice if you need to and don't let your expenses outweigh your income. If you aren't aware of the money and finances in your marriage right now, please do not feel ashamed; you are not alone. Many women do not know.

Marriages tend to have a routine to them, and many women do not know how much the bills or daily expenses are. So when the floor drops out and you are on your own, you may be shell shocked. That is why you want to have a good team in place to help you adapt and make changes suited to your lifestyle.

In the snap of a finger, your finances will end up your responsibility entirely. In addition to food and clothing, think about your mortgage/rent, car payment, power, heating and cooling, insurance, and any memberships you have. Those items can get expensive quickly, and if you do not learn how to manage your wealth, you will be one of those women who went broke in five years.

This overhaul can be emotionally taxing in addition to being expensive, and your financial advisor can be your best friend in that situation. They can help you plan out your budget and trim up any excess spending while you prepare for the long and possibly grueling process of divorce. You may need to sacrifice a few shopping trips and splurges while gearing up for the process, but hopefully you will not have to cut back forever.

Make a list of all your expenses so you can start to understand exactly what you spend money on. Sit down with your financial advisor and iron out the details so you are fully aware of the situation. Understanding each and every expense will allow you to get a big picture of the future ahead and what you need to do to not only survive but also thrive.

Do not estimate these costs. Having an exact dollar amount will best prepare you for when these expenses come around. A few dollars here and there quickly add up to hundreds, so take an honest look and be exact.

If you have children, do not forget to add in what your expenses are as far as they go. Children are expensive, so make sure to discuss with your spouse what will be taken care of and by whom. This discussion will allow you to know exactly how much money you need to sustain your kids' needs. Add these expenses to your detailed list, and do not forget books, school expenses, etcetera.

Any vacations or expenses such as entertainment must be factored into the equation, as well as miscellaneous expenses. Plan for these as far in advance as possible so you can budget around them and afford them without hurting yourself financially. Planning becomes much more important when you are on your own and in the middle of a divorce. That said, rekindling your independence is rewarding and can help you develop self-confidence.

When you sit down with your financial advisor, make sure you plan out a one-, three-, and five-year plan for your financial future. Take your time with this extensive list of finances because the more detailed you are now, the less surprises you will have later. This will give you a huge head start toward financial freedom and making sure that you stay afloat. Making this list will be one of the most important things that you will do to secure your financial future.

Plans are great, but without budgeting carefully, they are useless. Budgeting may well be the single most important thing you can learn to do during the process of divorce. Budgeting requires not only self-discipline but also sacrifice and creativity. Once you master the art of budgeting, your life will become more enjoyable as the stress of finances fades away.

Tips and Tricks

I learned some extremely useful tips about budgeting during my own learning process. The first is to live below your means if possible. Sure, a new pair of shoes sometimes feels great, but buying a new pair when they aren't needed may be a bit irresponsible. Living below your means is being able to pull back if you are typically a big spender and being honest about your finances.

What qualifies as living below your means is relative to your financial situation, but to establish a general rule, spend much less than you are used to when getting divorced. Not only will spending less than you are used to allow you to get an honest idea about what you need to survive, but reducing your spending will also encourage thinking before you spend. So much of what we buy is not essential. Getting a full understanding of what we are wasting our money on allows us to see the bigger picture.

My next tip may cause you to gasp. I need you to put away your credit cards for at least a year. Yes, no more racking up credit card bills. You may be wondering why, and it all comes down to spending money you do not have. During a divorce is no time to go into debt spending funds that are not really yours. Uncertainty is the only thing you have in abundance, and even though you have a good team, you want to make sure you protect yourself and your future.

Getting used to your baseline spending is the initial goal in a divorce. You may have no idea what your expenses are, and that is why you need to put away those credit cards. You need to get used to your spending pattern without the use of credit cards, because they often give you an easy out for splurging. Developing discipline and making things work without external sources of funding will allow you to acclimate to your true spending pattern. Unless you have an absolute emergency, please put away your credit cards and live below your means. And no, an extra pair of shoes is not an emergency. (I say this with love while laughing aloud.)

Another tip I learned is to work closely with your financial advisor. These experts will guide you to be able to budget everything you need to get through the divorce. Simply making a budget with them is not enough; you will have to follow through and stick to it. By working with your financial advisor, you will be able to draw up a weekly budgeting plan and strategize how much you would like to save and how much you can afford to spend. If you do not want to do a weekly plan and prefer to base expenses and savings around a monthly period, feel free to do so.

In drawing up a great plan with them, do not be afraid to ask questions. I was initially hesitant to ask questions to my financial advisor that I felt were embarrassing; however, I learned that the more that I knew, the better off I was for my long-term financial future.

You can learn a lot from these individuals, and they will be able to guide you as far as investments and savings plans go. Always remember that there is no such thing as a dumb question. This goes for repeating things as well. Do not nod your head and whiz through the meeting without understanding absolutely everything before you leave. You will feel much worse having to phone them up afterward and tell them you were not listening at the meeting, rather than asking them to repeat the information on the spot.

I also highly recommend that you document everything from the meetings with your financial advisor when you are going over your budget strategy, so invest in an inexpensive recorder. Phones these days may be able to do this, but you will want a recording device with a lot of space. A recorder will allow you to go back and access important information. If you want to take this documentation one step further, you can use a program such as Otter, which will transcribe voice to text and give you a manual you can abide by.

Another tip I would like to delve into is not stressing the difficulties of this process. Diving headfirst into daily expenses can be challenging if you were not responsible for them beforehand. At the very least, some things will be different than when you were with your spouse. Do not get upset if you make a mistake while getting used to the process, as your new situation will take some time to get used to. While this is the case, please do not go off the deep end and go on a stress-induced shopping spree. The faster you develop an understanding of what you need to be able to budget on a day-to-day basis, the better off your long-term financial future will be.

The detailed spreadsheet list I prompted you to make I meant to make this process simpler. A mistake here or there is understandable, as tracking everything you will need daily can be difficult. The idea is that you learn as you go until you have everything tuned up and you are confident about your budgeting abilities. This is one of the reasons we do not want to use credit cards, as we want a clear and disciplined approach to spending.

Did I mention the benefits of this entire process? As you manage and find yourself being able to budget, you will become more comfortable and confident in your independence. Anything about you that had been overshadowed by your spouse will find its way out again, and you will begin to shine brightly. But do not get too confident in your ability to manage money, as sticking close to discipline and abiding by the budget will keep you balanced and able to navigate any financial situation.

My last tip on budgeting is that you cannot be too careful. All expenses you can trim would be a great benefit to your budget during a divorce. The tighter you are financially and the less money moving out of your account, the more you can save. Being kind of careful is not enough when you are on your own. You must pay great attention to detail to ensure the puzzle fits together.

One way to expedite this process thanks to modern technology is to download a budgeting app. There are so many great apps out there that can track every dollar that you spend, so you do not have to note every single transaction manually. These apps are trusted by millions and will not sell your data or steal your identity; in fact, they make budgeting much easier for you. My philosophy is to make it easier on yourself." The process of divorce is already sticky and emotionally draining, and if you can have an app that tracks your budget for you, then you have one less thing to worry about.

As far as budgeting is concerned, it might be challenging right away. Discipline is key to getting exactly where you want to be, and the sooner you develop frugality, the sooner you will be able to breathe easier. The goal at the very least is to be able to live the lifestyle you had when you were in your marriage, and potentially even better. Budgeting gives you the ability to keep increasing the money in your account as opposed to decreasing, and this skillset is one of the building blocks of happiness through the divorce process.

Your Future Income

Let's now talk about how you will be bringing in your money. You need to figure out if you will need to work and where your money will be coming from.

If you were a homemaker and your spouse was the breadwinner, you must get access to every bank record possible and hire a forensic accountant. Getting this information could be crucial in setting yourself up financially for the type of lifestyle you want to live. If you are well off and will be receiving a hefty settlement, you might want to start talking to your financial advisor about where to invest those funds in a way that will fit your budget.

The topic of employment is crucial when it comes to divorce, so you have to start looking at your options. If you were not working when you were married, you might want to investigate potential jobs. Earning new income can be a great way to stay busy and help navigate your way through the emotional turmoil, while making additional income.

If you were working during your marriage and now during the divorce, you have most likely realized that your cost of living is much higher than you initially thought. As such, you may want to consider upgrading your education. I know the mere thought of going back to school and getting a higher degree can be a difficult proposition, but sometimes that path can be an adventurous new start and build your confidence. Also, learning new information and skills can be fun and raise your self-esteem during a time when your belief in yourself could have taken a hit because of the divorce.

Either way, you must think about employment and plan accordingly. Going back to school can cost money, so if you decide to pursue more education, make sure you investigate programs that offer financial assistance and will get you the most budget friendly option possible. If you are planning on starting a new career or job, make sure you pick one you will enjoy, and remember you will be emotionally vulnerable for a while because of the circumstances. Consult your coach and try to decide on a plan that is right for you based on what is happening around you.

Once you sit down with your financial advisor, a clearer picture will begin to take shape about what will be required for you to be able to sustain your preferred lifestyle. Having to work does not always mean that your life will be horrible as a result. Many jobs are fun and can take your mind off the stressful aspects of divorce. Making extra money never hurts the budget either, so working is usually a win-win.

Options are always available if you open your eyes and look for them. Think of all the tasks, hobbies, skills, and knowledge that you excel at, and you will have potential avenues you will be able to explore career-wise. You could open your own business, volunteer at places that you think are worthy of your time or explore other entrepreneurial routes. Assessments are available through psychologists that specialize in career development, and these can highlight areas that you would fit well in. You may look back and realize because of the divorce, you found your true calling.

Your Living Arrangements

The last topic that I would like to touch on as far as finances go is your house. You need to ask yourself where you want to end up living once you are divorced. Believe it or not, many women want to live in the house they were married in once they are divorced. This may seem strange, but surrounding yourself with what's familiar and comfortable, maintaining your daily life, and continuing to do things the way you are used to can create the desire to stay.

You may find yourself on the fence about staying in the house but consider a few variables before making this decision. I advise all my clients to remain open to the idea of moving out of the house and getting a fresh start. The house you lived in during your marriage contains a lot of memories that have the potential to cause you pain and suffering. A fresh start that includes you moving out and making new memories may make adjusting to your new normal easier for you. There are a lot of places (all but the place you lived in during your marriage) where new memories will come much easier, and you will not have memories of the past. You may want to consult with your financial advisor to understand what your options are before deciding one way or another. Talking this through with your coach is also recommended.

I want you to know that I was once one of those women who initially wanted to remain in my house after becoming divorced. Choosing which path to take was a difficult decision for me to make, and I almost ended up staying in the old house. However, I quickly realized I made the right decision to leave my marital home behind, move into a new house, and create many happy new memories. And I envisioned the move as a bridge to my newfound independence. I cultivated my confidence by having the courage to leave behind everything that was familiar and take a chance in a new place.

Leaving your marital home is not only a financial decision. Choosing a new home can potentially invite change into your life in a way that you might not think possible now. In a new place, you can create new patterns, new hopes, new memories, and new friends. Building yourself a new safe haven can initiate a time of growth in the face of great pain.

Another factor you need to consider when deciding to keep your old house is whether you can afford it. Property taxes are only going up, and the upkeep of the property can be extremely costly to maintain. Keeping up with all the work required around the property might take a lot of your time and energy, all while navigating emotionally troubling circumstances. If you can avoid putting yourself in an emotional and financial deficit, my advice is to do so. Starting fresh can seem daunting; however, if the house is much bigger than you need, your expenses would be better allotted elsewhere.

Not all memories in the old house are probably bad. If you have children, you probably have many fond memories of them growing up, so I understand the emotional stake that is probably weighing down on you. My advice is to not worry, because the kids will be okay, and so will you (see chapter four for details about how to help your kids through the divorce). Your financial and emotional well-being is much more important than memories, because remember that your children will always be your children, regardless of the place in which you live.

Think of all the benefits you might have moving into a new home or apartment. You can decorate and set up your home however you like best. You will be able to acquire new neighbors and friends, have a fresh outlook on new surroundings, and focus on creating excitement and joy moving forward. A fresh start may encourage you to develop a new skill or take up a new hobby, from growing your own patio tomatoes to rock climbing. Whatever you choose to pursue, use this opportunity to remind yourself that you can still explore, experiment, and try new things, and you may find the entire process of adapting much easier than before.

The line in the sand you must draw is whether or not you plan on keeping the house for the long term. If you want to keep it for only a few years, the house probably is not worth the trouble of trying to hold onto it during the divorce process. Remember, keeping or selling the house is not about sticking it to your spouse, but rather setting the table for your financial and emotional independence. If your plans for the house do not span into the far future, break away now, and save yourself the headache later.

This decision about your home is a touchy topic that you can discuss with your coach. Do not rush this decision, as there are huge financial and well-being ramifications in play. Make a list of pros and cons so that you can paint a clearer picture of whether keeping the house is worth it.

In certain circumstances, your spouse may also want the house, in which case you will want to consult your attorney. Remember that if you live in a 50/50 state, keeping the house will cost you a lot of potential assets, which means remaining in your marital home under those circumstances would fall under the con column of your list, rather than being a pro.

I cannot stress enough the importance of taking your time and weighing this decision carefully, as your living arrangements post-divorce can impact your outlook tremendously.

Chapter 3

Protect Your Wellness

E nough with the finances already. Let's dive into a topic that I really enjoy educating those going through divorces on, especially given that I am both a divorce and health coach. This chapter is ultimately the most important one in this book.

Hiring your people is important. Finances are important. But from this day forward, I want you to be one hundred percent aware that your health and wellness are what matter most. Granted, both of these should always be most important in our lives. Right now, however, these are critical for you.

To get through the lengthy and emotionally taxing process of divorce, you must have a clear state of mind. This means that every day you need to take care of yourself: your mind, body, and soul. If you do not have a wellness routine, you must start one. We will start slow. I'm not talking about gym memberships, and I'm not talking about running marathons. I'm talking about simple steps to start a basic routine.

Perhaps you already have a routine and are active in all three facets of the mind, body, and soul connection. Now is not the time to stop or slow that regimen. If anything, during times of crisis, you want to be twice as mindful as you usually are. You may find you have less energy because of the emotional vacuum that is divorce, but I assure you that if you push through and balance out this triad of well-being, you will be successful.

This will be a long chapter. I want to cover whether you have not started a wellness routine, or you currently have one but need to stay on track, because I want to make sure that you have a strong base to maintain your mental health.

Getting Started with Mindset and Nutrition

To start, it is paramount that you are in balance as far as your mental health goes. This can be achieved through being mindful, grateful, and thankful. Start your mornings with a routine that practices each of these important aspects and sets the tone for the day. One of my favorite quotes is as follows:

"Gratitude unlocks the fullness of life. It turns what we have into enough, and more. It turns denial into acceptance, chaos to order, and confusion to clarity. It can turn a meal into a feast, a house into a home, or a stranger into a friend. [...] Gratitude makes sense of our past, brings peace for today, and creates a vision for tomorrow."

– Melody Beattie, *The Language of Letting Go: Daily Meditations for Codependents*

This quote is especially useful to remind yourself that even though you are going through a hardship, you have it better than most. Consider what you have and remind yourself of the things that you can be grateful for, even in this difficult time. Some activities that you may find especially useful at the start of your day are a walk, meditation and prayer, yoga, essential oils, going to the gym, journaling, or simply eating a healthy breakfast.

Speaking of breakfast, now that you have a start to your wellness routine, I want to talk about the importance of eating healthily. Your nutrition is the basis for your energy levels, and during this time, you want to make sure you have enough energy to get through the divorce process. Doing a pantry makeover can be a great way to jumpstart your commitment to eating healthily and getting you on the right track.

Consider how often you look at the label of the food before you buy it. In terms of nutrition, we often take the brand's word at face value, throw our grocery items into the cart, and aimlessly consume the products. Many times, these foods end up taking energy from us rather than giving it. A bag of potato chips might encourage you to wallow in your sorrows on the couch, while an apple can give you a get-up-and-go boost. Nutrition can be everything in determining whether or not we choose to do something.

Having a cupboard full of energy rich foods is the basis for what I like to call my SEP self-care plan, which digs deep into our spiritual, emotional, and physical well-being. Proper nourishment will help all three of these pinnacles. Living a healthy lifestyle will encourage you in this time of trauma and allow you to grow and prosper. Your patience will increase, as well as your clarity and mental sharpness. Independence and understanding everything around you will follow. Let's dig deep and investigate how you can care for yourself using the SEP model.

Spiritual Well-being

Your spiritual strength needs to be higher than usual to get you through the taxing process of divorce. I am not saying that you should attend church if that is not for you, I suggest you be in touch with whatever energy you consider higher than your comprehension. I found by doing this regularly you can find peace within. Some activities you can do to help foster this connection include meditation, yoga, journaling, and even traveling.

Regarding the first, meditation is great for bringing yourself back to the center. At the basic level, meditation is paying attention to your breathing and trying to clear your head of all the thoughts that come to you during this moment of quiet.

When you first start practicing meditation, removing the clutter that filters into or bombards your mind as you breathe deeply may be difficult. My trick is to go to a dark place that is completely quiet and simply watch or visualize each breath on an individual basis. Slowly but surely each thought will start to quiet down, and eventually, with enough practice, you will be able to obtain clarity. Do not expect to become perfect on the first try, as those expectations will surely leave you disappointed.

The benefits of meditation are long proven, given the fact that this practice has been around for thousands of years. Meditation has been scientifically proven to show improvements in mindfulness and can help to clear out stress and anxiety. In a situation such as a divorce, improving your ability to be mindful in stressful situations is invaluable. When your STBX gives you a snide comment, you will be better able to shrug it off and keep your cool.

Meditation can be done in chunks of five, ten, or 15 minutes, and you can use it as needed. With enough practice, you might find yourself using several sessions a day to keep anxiety and stress at arm's length. Meditation is a great and free way to center yourself and get in touch with your spiritual side.

Yoga is another proven way to center yourself, as it is essentially meditation while exercising. During yoga, you will focus on both breathing and stretching, so you will get a workout while getting all the benefits of meditation. Yoga is a fantastic way to release stress and gently introduce yourself to the world of fitness if you have not already been acquainted.

Yoga is a great alternative to meditation if you find that you prefer moving instead of sitting still. Some people struggle with meditation because of its stationary nature; thus, they find that yoga enables them to achieve clarity faster through moving while focusing on their breathing. There are classes available at almost any gym, and if you do not want to get a gym membership, you can find plenty of videos online.

Journaling is a useful activity you can do to connect with your thoughts in a way that the spoken word cannot. I advise all my clients to journal daily about the thoughts and feelings they are having because journaling helps them to paint a clearer picture of their comprehensive mental health.

Sometimes journaling brings about hidden emotions and feelings they had not realized they were thinking. By finally bringing those hidden thoughts to the surface, you will be better able to address and even release them, so they won't weigh you down any longer. And during a divorce, being in touch with your thoughts, feelings, and emotions can strengthen your spirituality.

Writing about things that you are grateful for and making plans for the future are two ways you can build excitement as you look ahead. This process can help you to release the negative emotions and instead turn your attention to the good things that are coming up. Two journaling prompts that are useful when working toward this goal are writing a letter to yourself three years in the future and writing a thank you note to your higher power as you describe everything you are thankful for.

Traveling and exploring nature are the last two activities that I recommend that can assist your spiritual well-being. You may be scratching your head and wondering how you can afford to travel when you are supposed to be practicing new budgeting methods. I understand; traveling can be expensive.

But in terms of boosting your spirituality, I am not referring to the expensive variety of traveling. Find something that is surrounded by the blessings of nature which we have been given. Immersing yourself in nature can be a great way to find peace with your higher power and quell the stress and anxiety that has been bothering you. Take your kids for a hike or go camping somewhere that has trees, lakes, and stars, because spirituality is easy to find and connect with in these types of environments.

Spiritual strength ties into emotional well-being, so let's jump into it.

Emotional Well-being

Emotional strength is extremely important whether or not you are going through a divorce. You must protect your emotional well-being at all costs, because it can be fragile at times. During the process of divorce, every aspect of your emotional wellness is tested and can fall to pieces if you do not tend to it.

Even the people around you can impact your emotional well-being. That influence is why I encourage you to take charge, protect yourself, and set boundaries. Let people know exactly what is okay and what is not okay. Boundaries keep your emotional strength and well-being in a healthy state because you are empowering yourself. These boundaries could be with friends, family, and even your soon-to-be ex.

For example, you may want to tell your extended family that they are not to ask questions about your divorce in front of your kids, or your friends cannot trash talk about your ex because you do not want that constant, negative reminder triggering your anger. If somebody is not willing to respect the boundaries you create, you might want to think about not associating with them.

Hopefully they will get the picture and treat you how you want to be treated.

This step is especially important because divorces tend to make us emotionally vulnerable. Your self-worth has probably been damaged, and you are in a state of uncertainty, which can lead to emotional instability. Thus, creating boundaries is essential because they provide you with a comfort zone from which you can safely operate and allow you to rebuild yourself. If you fear hurting other people's feelings or offending them, swap that thought around, and remind yourself that they should want to protect and help you. Everybody you associate with should be mindful of what you will and will not tolerate, and they should want what is best for you. Setting boundaries is a surefire way to test who is really on your side, especially during this difficult time.

Creating solid boundaries sets the stage for the next phase of your life. Fear can hijack your emotional strength, so I want you to make sure that fear is not holding you back. Do not fear the past, and do not fear the future. Good things are ahead, and what is behind you is behind you. Live in the present and be mindful of the moment you are in now. Emotional strength is doing what you need to so that you can optimize your life. Fear has no place in the equation.

You may find it difficult to shake off the emotions of what is taking place with the divorce, and that is okay. Being honest with yourself and allowing yourself to feel these emotions is not a sign of weakness. The point is that you cannot let fear of the future ruin your ability to look forward to the adventures that lie ahead. Allow yourself to acknowledge that divorce is a painful experience. Giving yourself time to grieve is completely natural and healthy, so long as you know that you will get through this period fearlessly.

If you feel overwhelmed at times, know that it is okay to reach out. Many people tend to think that reaching out is a sign of weakness, so they keep their struggles all to themselves. Reaching out is actually a sign of emotional strength as opposed to weakness. Your trusted loved ones can help you navigate this process if you allow them to be there for you.

That said, make sure you reach out to people who respect your boundaries and give you positive energy to pave the way forward. Find your rocks in this journey and learn to consult them when you are not feeling your best. The idea is that they will rejuvenate you and encourage you to keep moving ahead.

The people whom you reach out to will not always be available, which is why hiring a therapist along the way is a good idea. Therapists are excellent resources. They can help get you on the right track because a qualified therapist can provide you with unbiased feedback and guide you through the emotional pitfalls of a divorce. In addition, they can help you to organize and process your thoughts so that you can move forward. The more often you can see your therapist, the better, because they are the emotional equivalent of a personal trainer.

Practicing mindfulness is just as useful for your emotional strength as for your spiritual strength. While you can use meditation to connect to your spiritual power, you can also use it to declutter your emotions. Let the emotions pass through you; give them their place, but do not cling to them. Feel the power of them as they pass through you, and you acknowledge them. This mindful practice will help you to not let your emotions build up and erupt like a volcano because they go unchecked.

You will have a lot of stressful situations moving forward, and the more balance you can approach them with, the better. A high level of emotional strength will allow you to handle them with grace as opposed to cursing in the courtroom. Restraint, patience, and clarity are all skills that can be strengthened by practicing mindfulness.

Another important aspect to building your emotional strength is allowing yourself to be vulnerable in certain situations. When dealing with a divorce, you most likely will want to close yourself off from the world and protect your emotions. This reaction is common.

However, shutting down emotionally is exactly the opposite of what you should do if you want to be healthy from here on out. By opening yourself up, you will learn what real love, sincerity, friendship, and trust feel like. If you had years of not receiving this in abundance, these feelings can be uncomfortable at first. I promise that if you sincerely open yourself up to others, you will find great joy and peace during this difficult journey.

In addition to opening yourself to others, learning to enjoy your own company is essential. Get to know that wonderful woman staring back at you in the mirror and realize how talented and beautiful you really are. When you are married, you often forget about your own needs and wants and how to enjoy your own company. During this process, you might feel strange or uncomfortable spending so much time with yourself, but the more you enjoy your own company, the better your healing will go for you. Mending your heart and emotions comes from inside, so warm up to yourself, and this process will be easier.

To help facilitate this, find a hobby you enjoy. If you do not know what you truly enjoy, revisit hobbies you used to have before you got married. Explore what you liked and did not like about those hobbies and if you would be interested in trying them again. You can also experiment with new hobbies until you find something that you love. Reigniting your passion will help you pass the time and distract yourself from the painful emotions that may try to work their way into your head. Play the piano, go for a walk, or join a yoga class. The possibilities are endless, and you can do a lot of fun things by yourself or with others who support you.

In line with enjoying your own company, remember to be gentle and kind to yourself. The main pillar of emotional strength comes from positive self-talk that creates positive energy and vibrations. A grueling divorce can lower your self-confidence and self-esteem, so build yourself up through affirmations that give you strength and empower you.

For example, look in the mirror and say out loud, "I am enough exactly as I am." This is a common, powerful affirmation, but you can practice more than one at a time. Choose affirmations that focus on who you want to be, such as "I am strong and confident. I remain calm when dealing with stressful situations." The more you repeat these affirmations, the sooner you will begin to not only believe them but also embody them.

Even if you may not think positively all the time, make sure that any critique of yourself has a positive twist on it for the best effect. Know your worth, and know you are in control of how you choose to address yourself. In your marriage, you probably felt you had lost control, and in turn you stopped talking about yourself kindly. You must change how you speak to yourself to rebuild your emotional strength.

Know that your emotions manifest themselves in many ways. In this sense, you must take control of your body language and make sure that it reflects positivity. Many of my clients came to me with poor body language that projected defeat and low self-esteem. Once they reclaimed their body language, they stood proudly and projected strength, clarity, and ambition. What you project will manifest itself into reality, so make sure that you are carrying yourself well.

Above all else, avoid drama. The reason we seek to set boundaries and surround ourselves with good energy is to improve our emotional strength. Those who partake in drama want to sap all that good energy and cause you to become more stressed and anxious than you already are. At the first hint of drama, withdraw yourself from the situation, and tell whomever is responsible that they crossed your boundary. They will get the picture and switch the subject to more relevant topics, or they must find somebody else to spew drama to. You need to steer clear of those who chum the waters with drama so that you can grow stronger emotionally.

Physical Strength

Now that we have your spiritual and emotional strength in place, let's talk about your physical strength. While this chapter pertains to your physical body, you do not need to build yourself up so that you can compete in a bodybuilding competition anytime soon (unless that is your thing, of course).

What I mean by physical strength is developing a connection with your body that can help you gain clarity and confidence in your presence. Physical activity during a divorce is imperative because studies show that exercise can help fend off the anxiety and depression that often come with overwhelming emotions.

If you do not have a gym or exercise routine, now is a great time to begin one. Some of the benefits of starting a routine include building confidence in your body, mental clarity, a boost in cognition, honing your discipline, and an overall feeling of well-being. Did you know that when you partake in exercise, you release endorphins that rival the chemicals released by painkillers? Essentially, physical activity is your medication throughout this grueling process and can help calm your nerves and build patience. Combine that with eating healthy and practicing emotional and spiritual strength, and you will become an unstoppable force.

Feeling good about yourself will boost your confidence and self-esteem, which can be damaged during a long and unfruitful marriage. Physical activity will help with your self-worth and allow you to remember how stunning and beautiful you are. My clients that start fitness routines report considerable improvements in all aspects of their life and are always happier than when they did not integrate physical activity into their routine.

Start the process slowly. You do not immediately need to buy a gym membership and turn into a fitness superstar. If your budget allows for those resources, then hiring a personal trainer to guide you through the initial phases of your fitness routine can be extremely helpful. You can also try apps on your phone that can put together similar routines if your budget cannot accommodate a trainer.

If you want to start even slower and do not feel that weights are necessary, you can choose a variety of different activities that do not require a trainer, or you can try free apps that will get your body moving. These activities include walking, biking, hiking, swimming, climbing stairs, dancing, working out with resistance bands, tai chi, simple stretching, and Pilates. Every one of these activities will be a great addition to your routine, and you will begin feeling the benefits almost immediately.

The reason I am so big on developing a fitness routine is because during the divorce process, you will have bad days. They are inevitable, and you will need a healthy outlet for your frustration and a designated way to recenter yourself. Having a go-to physical activity will help you to develop patience and build your physical strength at the same time. By making spiritual and emotional progress while developing your fitness routine, there will be no obstacle you cannot get through.

However, you may be wondering why you should implement a fitness routine now if it has never been a part of your life prior to your divorce. My answer is that you want to put into place now anything that will help you succeed in the future. Use this time of pain to facilitate growth and become a better version of yourself than ever. A fitness routine will help to foster independence and confidence, and you will feel yourself becoming more powerful than you ever could have imagined.

Creating a Better Future

Each of these three strengths serve a purpose in helping you to build up your stamina so that you can get through this divorce and be better off than you were before. Every adaptation of behavior that you put into place now will leave you stronger than ever, and you may come out of the divorce feeling more confident than you have ever been. I place value on this time being a period of great growth and new experiences. Remember that you can find tools that can help you hone each area of strength, including personal trainers, therapists, and spiritual teachers such as yogis and gurus.

Keep in mind that you have a budget to focus on. Even though self-care is the most important facet of going through divorce, splurging on things that you cannot afford will not be beneficial to your future.

Tie all three of these areas together to become the strongest version of yourself. Each area is related to the other two, I recommend that you avoid developing only one and neglecting the others, or they all will come undone. Build a strong base within each strength, and then further develop one at a time and at a pace you are comfortable with. Soon enough, you will be feeling better than you have in a long time.

Chapter 4

Helping Your Kids

One of the most pressing issues that you may be having is how the kids will react to the divorce. I got divorced after 20 years of marriage, and our kids were my biggest concern throughout the entire divorce process. However, I feel like I could have handled our divorce better emotionally speaking, and that is why I would love to pass some knowledge on to you and allow you to handle your divorce in a way that will have the least amount of impact on your children.

As I said before, your children will be okay, but they will struggle through this transition. And no matter what you do to try to prevent this, depending on your children's ages and what they have endured during the rocky ending to your marriage, they are going to feel sad. The most important thing to remember is that you are doing this for them by removing yourself from the situation that is causing you pain and preventing you from being the best mother possible. Stepping away from a rocky marriage while still putting the children first takes courage, but with proper steps, you can become a better mother than ever before.

Supporting Their Well-Being

The first step is to reassure your children that everything will be okay. Be transparent and honest with them about what is taking place. Although telling the truth may hurt a little, in the end they will thank you for your transparency. Tell them you want to be the best mother possible to them, and good things are coming because of the divorce. Your attitude toward the process will determine their level of comfort with what is taking place. Remaining composed and put together will assure them that you and they will be okay and that you have everything under control.

In times of turmoil like divorce, it is important to remember that your children view you as a leader; thus, you must lead by example. Falling off and becoming a puddle of tears will make them feel vulnerable and alone, and that could lead to problems down the road. Keeping calm, building yourself up, and gaining momentum will show them that this is a time for growth and will signal to them to chase their dreams and desires. How you carry yourself has everything to do with how they will carry themselves, so make sure you set a good example.

Encourage them in all their proactive pursuits to show that you are supportive and are still putting them first despite the less than desirable situation. If they decide to participate in a sport, make sure you are in the front row if time permits. They will see that you are more focused than ever on their well-being and feel comfortable growing. Let them know you are there for any questions they have and that you will be truthful and honest with them. You are still their biggest fan, and in being supportive of them, you will help ease your own stress and anxiety.

Remember that you are the parent, and they are the child, so try not to lean on them when you are feeling vulnerable. If they see you struggling emotionally, make sure they know they are not responsible for your happiness and that, although you feel sad at times, you can handle yourself. Hug them and show love to them. Accept the love they show you; however, do not put the burden on your children, as they are already going through enough.

Your therapist and close friends are the ones you want to confide in most, not your children. I have seen divorces create parents who end up turning their children into the adults while the parents pick themselves up, and that is counterproductive for your children's health.

Keep the Kids Neutral

In relation to remembering that you are a parent to your child, make sure to never put them in the middle of the divorce process and that they never become a mediator between you and your ex. This puts a tremendous amount of stress on your children, and they end up feeling like they are a pawn that is used to deliver messages back and forth. This will cause them to stop pursuing their own passions and end up stunting their social and emotional growth.

Keep the divorce as far as possible from your relationship with your children. If they ask you specific questions about what is taking place, be transparent but positive. This will establish that you are in control of your emotions and that you are focusing on becoming the best parent you can possibly be to them. This strength relates to the first point about the way your children look to you as a leader. Never put your children in a me-or-your-father scenario. Forcing this choice on them will cause unbelievable amounts of stress in your children and will do more damage than anything else during this process.

You are still a family, just not a family under one roof. Being civil and supporting your children and their relationship with their father is paramount to any ill will you feel because of the divorce. You and your ex may have done or said many horrible things; however, the most important thing is being mature and prioritizing and protecting your child's welfare throughout this situation. Your therapist can be your venting system, along with your fitness and mindfulness routine.

I cannot stress enough the importance of not making your children bargaining chips or messengers who do your bidding. So many parents end up doing this and do untold damage to their children in this fragile time frame. Your children could end up withdrawing from their social circles and suffering from mood disorders, anxiety, or depression if you put them in the middle.

If you suspect your ex is doing this to your children, tell your attorney immediately, as your ex's behavior puts them at risk. My philosophy is taking the high road at all costs because the welfare of your children is more important than any disagreement or the desire to volley distasteful messages back and forth. If you position yourself as the mature and respectful parent and your ex is playing below the belt, you will have more grounds for taking the children into your custody. In addition to not making your children choose between your ex and you, try not to create conflicting plans where the children would want to be in both spots at the same time. Organize things with your ex to try and make time spent with each of you optimal in the activity of your choosing. If you hear that your child has an event scheduled that your ex would usually attend, do not plan something enticing to try to pry your child over to your side. This manipulation is not beneficial to your children; instead, they will feel like they are missing out and will not be able to enjoy their original plans. Revel in your children's joy, not your ex's misfortune, no matter what wrongdoing your ex did to you during the marriage.

Treat the children as you always have, only better. This doesn't mean that you want to spoil them, as children are smart and will figure out that you are trying to make it up to them. Instead of showering them with material possessions, support all their ambitions and be more present with them daily. Encouragement is the best way to prove to them that you are taking the initiative in a more positive way than ever before.

Involve them in Planning the Future

In keeping consistent with allowing yourself to be vulnerable, share with them the opinions you have been considering for your future and demonstrate constructive feedback that they can use to shape themselves. Make sure they feel as if they are priority number one, and you can do this by offering the most valuable commodity you have to them, which is your time and attention.

Opening up to them about your future plans will go a long way in allowing them to trust that you will be there for them. Giving them input on how you should go about approaching the future will build excitement for all of you and give you something to look forward to.

If a job is in your future, be direct and explain to your children that you will be working more often but will still be available to make sure that their every need is met. Ask them where they envision living and listen to the suggestions they have, because when your children feel heard, that level of communication brings you closer together.

If they are younger, make sure to encourage them about all the amazing things you will be able to do together. Think of new ideas on how you can have fun and embark on adventures that you haven't previously. For example, go for walks to explore the neighborhoods and their playgrounds you are considering moving to. Or ask your children what they want to learn how to cook, even if that's chocolate chip waffles from scratch, and make those together.

Show your children that this change is a time for growth and opportunity and that everything is going to work out. If they are older, they may already have established circles of friends whom they would not want to move away from. Factor this in before making a huge move that would pull them away, as this could result in added stress. You may have to make sacrifices; however, do not compromise your own happiness to the degree that you are willing to be miserable to accommodate your children's preferences. Find a happy medium and meet in the middle.

Guilt Doesn't Help

Guilt is a powerful emotion you might be tempted to feel during this process. Let that pain go and show yourself compassion. You are escaping a situation that over time would have only gotten worse, and you are sustaining the courage to change the situation. That determination is something that you cannot feel guilty about, because your intent is to make both you and your children happier. Remaining part of the status quo and tolerating a situation that is making you miserable is not going to be beneficial for anyone.

Your children would not want you to feel guilty, so those feelings are often coming from the self-defeating voice inside the back of your head whispering sweet nothings. Try to establish boundaries even with this little voice, and do not allow it to churn the feelings of guilt and angst in your psyche. Tell your therapist about these feelings, so you can create a plan on how to sufficiently deal with them. This is a time to feel empowered, not guilty.

Conflict with your Ex

The toughest part of going through a divorce with children is that certain things will no longer be the same. The children will live going back and forth, to and from each parent, given that both parents want to maintain an active role in their children's lives. This constant interaction will require both you and your ex to be on cordial terms so that you can do these pick up and drop offs to the best of your abilities.

If you do not know how to address this with your ex, a good place to start the conversation is with something along the lines of, "Let's make sure we get along as best as we can for the children's sake." Work with your ex in facilitating a positive environment for your children because being cordial makes family events and interactions so much easier than being hostile with one another.

Certain points of the divorce may get ugly, especially if you have a bitter ex who wants to spite you. You must roll with the punches and document everything to make the best case. Do not feed into your ex's games if he chooses to play them, and make sure you are on the high road. I know it's hard to breath up there sometimes but it's the best route to take

One last note about the conflict with your ex: Make sure you report everything to your attorney. Anything you say to your ex can be used against you when the court decides who gets custody and visitation. You must be on your best behavior during the entire process to ensure that you and your children will be able to be together. I assure you, taking every precaution during this grueling process will be worth it, and you can do it!

This type of situation is why I am so big on the spiritual, emotional, and physical self-care system. Maintaining your wellness builds self-control and instills values within you that will allow you to have the stamina to navigate choppy waters. You will be able to take refuge in your newfound strength, instead of engaging in a tit-for-tat game of hostility.

The Big Picture

In summary, your children should always come first. During this difficult time, be mindful and move with intention. Set an example that you can be proud of, and let your children know you and they will be okay. Be supportive and encourage them to help you make plans for the future. Assure them that you are still a family, even though you do not live in the same home together.

Try to get on civil grounds with your ex for the sake of the children, and do not put the children in the middle of the firestorm. If it gets ugly and your ex decides they do not want to play by these rules, consult your attorney instead of reacting to your ex so that the court grants you the best results.

If you need a divorce coach who has been through this war of attrition, I can be in your corner in an instant.

Chapter 5

What Comes Next

"What comes next after divorce?" you may ask. Well, it all depends on what you have put into place *during* the process. Hopefully by this time your routines are in full swing, and your spiritual, emotional, and physical health are better than they have ever been. I hope the divorce went smoothly, your kids are not only doing well but also happier than before, and you have enough assets to be comfortable continuing the lifestyle that you are used to having.

If you followed this guide to get to this point, you are probably in a better spot than when you started the divorce and have the edge on ninety-nine percent of women who go through the same process. Awesome job. Let's talk about what comes next.

Future Relationships

Healing is something that will be ongoing for the rest of your life. When looking toward future love interests you may laugh and say that you are never going through that again. I do not blame you. I said the same thing myself, but now I am happily remarried and thriving.

Taking the time to develop and nurture yourself and build up those new foundations so that you can enter a place where you are happy and comfortable in your own company is the key to being able to become open to new relationships. You will most likely have a wall between you and anyone who would like to get close to you, and why you erected that wall is completely understandable. However, remember that allowing yourself to be vulnerable and honest will make forming new relationships easier with time as you learn to trust again.

Designate the initial time after the divorce to heal all the areas where you were hurt. This includes taking back control of your physical strength, emotional strength, and spiritual strength. Continue to follow the techniques in each area to build up these areas and find new and creative ones that add value to you. This may be a slow process, and everyone's journey to finding peace and healing is unique to them. Seeing your therapist at least once a week will allow you to gauge your progress and continue to grow.

Amending all relationships that the divorce process damaged is a great way to level the field and start fresh. You might not have been in the best state of mind during most of that difficult time and reaching out to let those whom you may have hurt know that you are truly sorry is a cleansing endeavor.

Rebuild your base of trusted loved ones stronger than ever and let them know you are doing a complete overhaul of your life from a spiritual, emotional, and physical standpoint. They may even want to join one of your activities, and you will have partners on your journey.

Finding Purpose

Once you have a great head start on healing yourself and amending the relationships that you or the divorce may have damaged, you should look toward your goal of self; that is, find a purpose. You may already know exactly what you want to do with your time from this point on, in which case, you are ahead of the curve. If you are uncertain about what you would like to purposely work toward, try journaling or discussing options with your coach or therapist to find out what may call to you.

You can find a purpose through three specific activities that I suggest to all my clients after they have nearly completed the lengthy process of divorce, so that as their cases near completion they can start to look for possibilities. The first of these activities is meditation, which I explained in more detail in chapter 3 under the "Spiritual well-being" section.

First and foremost, meditation will help you to quiet your mind and heal from the wounds of your divorce. As a secondary benefit, you will have the clarity to find what truly matters to you and is worth pursuing. Living out your dreams is never too late, and meditation can identify exactly what those are.

Listen to what the universe has to say to you while meditating. Usually, we speak to the universe and do not give it a chance to talk. You need a great deal of patience and to find a place free of distractions to hear what the universe has to say. If you listen closely, it may point you in a direction that you never would have been able to identify.

The second activity that can help you to identify purpose is giving back. This can come through volunteering at local organizations such as homeless shelters and animal shelters. Volunteering can help you to not only develop a sense of purpose but also heal the wounds that you went through in your marriage and divorce. Even a few hours of your time given to the right cause that makes you feel needed and valued can set into place a series of events that will help you visualize the rest of your life.

Giving back can also come in the form of joining organizations that facilitate building friendships and doing good around the community. The comradery of volunteer groups can help you build a network of like-minded individuals who are united for a cause, which in turn can result in forging some amazing friendships. Some of these groups include charities as well as organizations that offer opportunities for students around the community. Do a little research and find a way to give back in whatever way you can.

The third activity, which is also my favorite, is taking a class or joining a hobby group. Doing this allows you to not only expand your mind and creativity but also develop new skills that you never knew you had the potential to learn. The world is your oyster and joining a hobby club or a group can help uncover passions in waiting. Some groups or classes that you could potentially join include art, fashion, poetry, gardening, sewing, painting, pottery, teaching, writing, sports, running, or science.

The number of these types of clubs and groups are endless. You just need to put yourself out there, be open to trying new activities, and find the ones that keep you motivated and generate excitement.

When you are in a failing marriage, you can feel like the world around you is crumbling, which can cause you to retreat from the amazing resources your community offers. Perhaps you never tried many of these activities because your relationship consumed you and your desire to try new things. But now is the time to discover what truly makes you tick and what your passions truly are. Nobody can tell you what you can and cannot do, so taking initiative is key in this situation.

Not everyone is an extrovert, and that is completely okay. Clubs or hobbies based on individualistic growth are perfect for introverts as well. You can join these clubs and take classes virtually. The important part is that they keep you busy and help develop your purpose.

If you feel courageous, step outside of your comfort zone, and sign up for something that would usually be considered out of your element. This kind of challenge is where even more growth happens. Putting yourself in a position where you are uncomfortable will force you to adapt. What can be painful at first ends up being like a cold and refreshing dive into a crystal-clear pool. Many of my clients have told me that when they stepped out of their comfort zone, they found their true purpose—not a moment sooner, and not a moment later. When they dive in headfirst, they find what makes them tick.

As I went over in the previous chapter, do not let fear undermine your future. Divorce is one of the most stressful times that you can go through, but you made it. You took the high road, developed strength in the three core areas of your life (spiritual, emotional, and physical strength), and you paved the way for your children to live in a safe and stable environment.

Fear was not strong enough to stop you during this process, so do not let it creep into your life now that you are home free. You deserve to live a life that is full of meaning and purpose, and you will find everything and more if you have faith in yourself.

Now that your divorce case is closed, do not stop what you have built throughout the divorce process. Everything that you have learned and put into practice will allow you to continue to grow each day. Attack life with the same fervor that you did through this process, and you might find that you are making an even more comfortable living and have much more good energy and loved ones surrounding you. I am not saying that your divorce has been the best thing that ever happened to you, but everything does happen for a reason.

If you are worried that you have not found your purpose or calling, do not fret. The less you think about chasing those goals and forcing them to materialize, the more likely they will find you when you least expect. The key is to remain busy and try out everything you have ever wanted to try. The more things you experience, the more opportunities you will have for something to capture your imagination.

Avoid Learning the Hard Way

Please know that everything I have laid out for you, I have been through myself. I was responsible for finding my team members, and I had to figure out that process without any assistance, which often left me feeling alone and overwhelmed. I could have used some guiding light and experience. Emotionally, I was a mess and didn't know who to turn to for support. I struggled to figure out how to help myself, let alone my kids. As a result, my relationship with my children took a hit too, and I couldn't find the balance I once had. All I knew was that I needed to get out of my marriage and find a way to turn my life all around.

Each and every step in the process that I have given you in this book is based on the lessons I learned after making mistakes. One of my gifts that I have recognized post-divorce is that I learn from my mistakes, and sharing my story and experience with others is partly how I give back so that other women do not make the same mistakes.

Too many women out there are struggling to find help through this terrifying process, and society does not provide enough resources to help guide those women to salvation. I am greatly honored to be able to help them learn through my knowledge of the subject. If you are struggling to find your way through this difficult situation, know that you can find resources that will help you get through to the other side and grow from this experience.

I cannot stress enough the importance of a great divorce coach. Think of a sports team without a great leader. They may have all the talent in the world, but if nobody can steer the ship, all the talent in the world can fall through the cracks. Until recently, hiring a divorce coach was not commonplace, and sadly, women usually end up getting the short end of the stick in divorce.

I have talked to so many women who have tried to navigate this process alone, and they have told stories about them losing control of their health, happiness, and peace of mind. Their attorneys end up doing a half-asked job for their female clients. They lose track of their budget and forget to hire key members of their team. The result is that women get less than they deserve, become unhappy with their self-image, and damage their relationship with their children.

During the process, some women feud with their ex, and of course they pay for this when the judge doesn't give them custody. Divorce can take everything from a woman, and not having the proper plan in place can be the difference between everything and nothing.

This all can be prevented by having the right divorce coach to handle the process for you. While you will have to still be disciplined and balanced, having somebody on your team, someone who has been where you are and has learned the ins and outs over many years, is priceless.

I am not saying that you should hire me, but I do want you to find a divorce coach who can put this whole puzzle together for you. From the moment the divorce begins, every decision you make is crucial, and having the right person whom you can consult will help you immensely. This coach should not only handle all the difficult team hiring aspects but also tell you what to say and what not to say. They should act as a life coach during this turbulent time and be your eyes and ears in the trenches. They should be somebody whom you can talk to about absolutely anything and be able to understand where you are coming from. You do not need to learn the hard way because a great divorce coach has already done the research for you.

I remember getting done with my divorce and making a list of everything that I would have done differently during the process. I thought for days on end about whom I would have hired to make my life easier for the divorce. I could have avoided all the mistakes and extra stressors and anxiety, and I documented how each and every aspect could have been improved. At that point, I had also developed a system for myself that ensured my spiritual, emotional, and physical health, but I have now fine-tuned that system so that it is now optimized for the duration of the divorce process. As I wrote pages and pages of material, I realized I did not want any more women to go through what I had just endured. In doing so, I had found my purpose.

After years of studying and perfecting my methods and then sharing them with those who were going through what I had, I decided to become a divorce and life coach. Many of my friends whom I helped through the process insisted that I needed to pursue coaching as a career because if I kept my experience to myself, I was doing a disservice to the women out there who were alone and lost. I listened to them and took my talents to the coaching world, and I am proud to help women get exactly what they deserve while improving their lifestyles.

If you are reading this and trying to follow each step but are finding roadblocks in your way, I can help you get through each one with grace and strength. I will help organize and coordinate each facet of the SEP system and make sure you achieve exactly what you have in mind. If we do this process together, you can be sure that you will never be alone again. The process can be difficult, but having somebody on your team who has an arsenal of talent can make this process extremely smooth.

We will let the professionals handle everything that falls within their wheelhouse while we work on your SEP plan together. My life coaching methods will help you develop yourself while undergoing the grueling process of divorce. Your children will be amazed at your transformation, as will family and friends who will witness it. We will build your confidence together and attack this situation instead of playing defense the whole time and ending up with less than you deserve.

Once the process is underway, I will help keep you accountable as far as budget and self-care goes. Accountability is useful in that you will feel tied to something greater than yourself, and because of that, you will stick with it. Slip-ups happen but are much less frequent if somebody is guiding you toward the finish line. We will work on your ability to meditate and practice mindfulness to gain control of your emotions and help reestablish your spiritual essence. My personal goal for all my clients is to have them to be in the best shape of their lives at the same time they are going through their divorce. Many coaches would say that is too much to ask of their clients, but my clients are strong and empowered women, so we do not listen to what anybody else says.

After the divorce goes smoothly and you are finished with the process, I will help you discover passion and purpose. Most coaches leave after the divorce is complete, but I believe coaching is a process that continues far after the divorce is done. If you decide you want to change careers or go into something unique and inspiring, I will be there every step of the way for you. My experience with helping clients to find unique opportunities in which they can channel their purpose is what separates me from the rest, and I would love to do the same for you.

In conclusion, I hope this guide has helped calm your nerves and given you a starting point. I also want you to believe that, despite this process being difficult, a fresh start is on the way. I would absolutely love to hear from you and be part of your journey in creating a new and exciting chapter in your life. Everything that you could ask for in a partner during this process is only an email away. I hope you take the initiative to get started.

Healing is an active process, and you must be ready to do the work. I can only guide you.

Acknowledgments

A huge heartfelt THANK YOU to

Maria Secoy & the Allwritewell team for making this process easy and enjoyable. Maria, you have been so easy to work with.

To my family and friends who have always encouraged me to keep doing what I'm doing. The support is heartfelt.

To Christina Denali – What I have learned from you is valuable –

I appreciate you significantly. I hope we meet one day.

To all of the magnificent women I have met in the last couple of years. Your drive and passions inspire me

To MM for your love and support - much love to you, babe.

My kids, who I love to the moon and beyond. I am so proud of each of you. I hope I make you proud as well.

About Author

Nanette had been married for nearly twenty-five years when she divorced. Over those twenty-five years, She became the mother of three children. Over the years, she was a Household Engineer. This included being a transportation specialist, director of the accounts payable, cleaning lady, laundry specialist, short order cook, banker, bookkeeper, bedtime storyteller, and fashionista creator. Nanette became a certified Life and Health Coach in 2020. In addition, Nanette was also a driving instructor, part-time/full-time teacher, coach, counselor, and mentor.

The adjustments were challenging as Nanette transitioned into single life and became a single parent. Still, she gained strength, confidence, and courage to become the woman she had always known she could be. As a result, Nanette became a published author of the book Shattered Dreams

& New Beginnings: Her journey of heartbreak, healing, and growth. She is also part of two other multi-author books.

Nanette found her strength after heartbreak, discovered her drive after healing, and now knows her purpose because of her growth. Now, she follows her passion as a Divorce & Health Coach for women rediscovering their independence after decades of marriage.

Her divorce was long and painful, but she learned a lot. She not only survived it, but now she is thriving. Nanette learned to manage all her finances, which enabled her to preserve her lifestyle. Her goal is to coach, support, and mentor other women to do the same.

One of Nanette's long-time passions is giving back. She is drawn to charities helping children of all ages. She has been a Co-chair on a committee for a local charity raising money for children who live in a shelter for homeless families. She has been involved with this charity on many different levels for nearly 20 years.

She was recently asked to join a committee for another local charity that grants wishes to sick children in Michigan. Nanette was very grateful for this request and is loving it.

Learn More about How I Can Help

Divorce is life changing, and it can be even more traumatic if you are not supported.

I coach women divorcing after decades of marriage.

I have seen so many women struggle with regret because they did not take the proper steps to prepare for divorce.

I am committed to helping you:

- Prepare
- Guide you through this process
- Implement a plan
- Focus on your self-care
- Survive your divorce

- Set goals for your future

Help is here; you do not have to go through this journey alone. I promise it will get better. Let me help you through this painful time in your life.

Ease your stress and anxiety, and have no regrets.

Connect with Me:

https://www.facebook.com/groups/3293168907579186

https://www.instagram.com/divorcecoachingwithnanette/

https://www.twitter.com/@NDMurphy65

nanettemurphy@divorcecoachingwithnanette.com

https://www.livelifenowwithpurpose.com

www.ingramcontent.com/pod-product-compliance
Lightning Source LLC
Chambersburg PA
CBHW050751160726
48004CB00002B/506